THE

NEGRO'S COMPLAINT:

A POEM.

TO WHICH IS ADDED,

PITY FOR POOR AFRICANS.

BY WILLIAM COWPER.

London:

PRINTED FOR HARVEY AND DARTON,

GRACECHURCH-STREET.

1826.

THE
NEGRO'S COMPLAINT.

FORCING A NEGRO FROM HIS HOME.

———

Forc'd from home and all its pleasures,
Afric's coast I left forlorn;
To increase a stranger's treasures,
O'er the raging billows borne.

THE ARRIVAL IN THE WEST INDIES.

Men from Europe bought and sold me,
Paid my price in paltry gold;
But, though slave they have enroll'd me,
Minds are never to be sold.

THE TORTURE.

—

Still in thought as free as ever,
What are England's rights, I ask,
Me from my delights to sever,
Me to torture, me to task?

THE APPEAL.

Fleecy locks and black complexion
    Cannot forfeit Nature's claim;
Skins may differ, but affection
    Dwells in white and black the same.

THE NEGRO'S LABOUR.

Why did all-creating Nature
    Make the plant, for which we toil?
Sighs must fan it, tears must water,
    Sweat of ours must dress the soil.

THE MASTER'S CAROUSAL.

—

Think, ye masters iron-hearted,
Lolling at your jovial boards;
Think how many backs have smarted
For the sweets your cane affords.

THE ADDRESS.

———

Is there, as you sometimes tell us,
   Is there one, who reigns on high?
Has he bid you buy and sell us,
   Speaking from his throne the sky?

THE PUNISHMENT.

Ask him, if your knotted scourges,
    Matches, blood-extorting screws,
Are the means that duty urges
    Agents of his will to use?

THE TORNADO.

Hark! he answers—wild tornadoes,
   Strewing yonder sea with wrecks;
Wasting towns, plantations, meadows,
   Are the voice, with which he speaks.

THE WHIRLWIND.

He, foreseeing what vexations
    Afric's sons should undergo,
Fix'd their tyrant's habitations
    Where his whirlwinds answer—no.

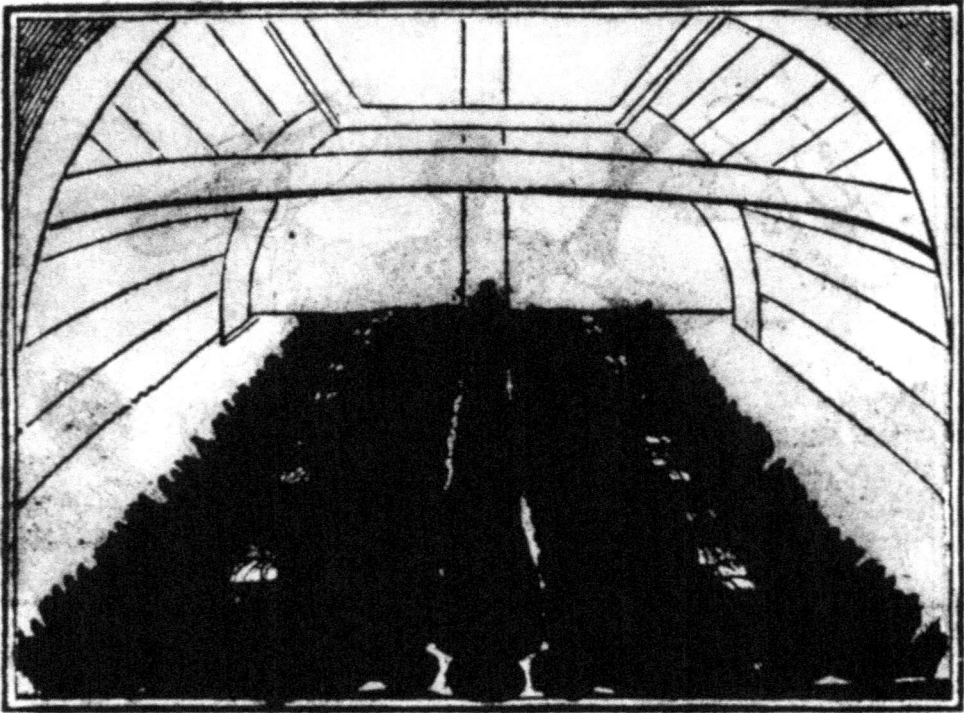

THE SLAVE-SHIP.

———

By our blood in Afric wasted,
    Ere our necks receiv'd the chain;
By the mis'ries that we tasted,
    Crossing in your barks the main;

THE SLAVE-MARKET.

By our suff'rings, since ye brought us
To the man-degrading mart ;
All, sustain'd by patience, taught us
Only by a broken heart :

RATIONAL PIETY.

———

Deem our nation brutes no longer,
Till some reason ye shall find
Worthier of regard, and stronger
Than the colour of our kind.

BARGAINING FOR SLAVES.

Slaves of gold, whose sordid dealings
Tarnish all your boasted pow'rs,
Prove that you have human feelings,
Ere you proudly question ours!

PITY FOR POOR AFRICANS.

1.

I own I am shock'd at the purchase of
 slaves,
And fear those who buy them and sell them
 are knaves ;
What I hear of their hardships, their tor-
 tures, and groans,
Is almost enough to draw pity from stones.

2.

I pity them greatly, but I must be mum,
For how could we do without sugar and
 rum?
Especially sugar, so needful we see?
What, give up our desserts, our coffee, and
 tea !

3.

Besides, if we do, the French, Dutch, and
    Danes,
Will heartily thank us, no doubt, for our
    pains;
If we do not buy the poor creatures, they
    will,
And tortures and groans will be multiplied
    still.

4.

If foreigners likewise would give up the
    trade,
Much more in behalf of your wish might be
    said;
But, while they get riches by purchasing
    blacks,
Pray tell me why we may not also go
    snacks?

5.

Your scruples and arguments bring to my
mind

A story so pat, you may think it is
coin'd,

On purpose to answer you, out of my
mint;

But I can assure you I saw it in print.

6.

A youngster at school, more sedate than
the rest,

Had once his integrity put to the
test;

His comrades had plotted an orchard to
rob,

And ask'd him to go and assist in the
job.

7.

He was shock'd, sir, like you, and an-
    swer'd—'Oh no!

What! rob our good neighbour! I pray
    you don't go;

Besides, the man's poor, his orchard's his
    bread,

Then think of his children, for they must
    be fed.'

8.

' You speak very fine, and you look very
    grave,

But apples we want, and apples we'll
    have;

If you will go with us, you shall have a
    share,

If not, you shall have neither apple nor
    pear.

9.

They spoke, and Tom ponder'd— 'I see
 they will go;
Poor man! what a pity to injure him
 so!
Poor man! I would save him his fruit if
 I could,
But staying behind will do him no
 good.

10.

'If the matter depended alone upon
 me,
His apples might hang, till they dropp'd
 from the tree;
But, since they will take them, I think I'll
 go too,
He will lose none by me, though I get a
 few.

11.

His scruples thus silenc'd, Tom felt more
at ease,
And went with his comrades the apples
to seize;
He blam'd and protested, but join'd in the
plan:
He shar'd in the plunder, but pitied the
man.

THE END.

Harvey, Darton, and Co. Printers,
Gracechurch-Street, London.

www.ingramcontent.com/pod-product-compliance
Lightning Source LLC
Chambersburg PA
CBHW081453070426
42452CB00042B/2719